ITSM

QuickStart Guide

The Simplified Beginner's Guide to IT Service Management

ClydeBank
TECHNOLOGY

Edition # 1 – Updated : September 15, 2016

Editors : Marilyn Burkley and Patricia Guth

Cover Illustration and Design: Katie Poorman, Copyright © 2016 by ClydeBank Media LLC
Interior Design: Katie Poorman, Copyright © 2016 by ClydeBank Media LLC

ClydeBank Media LLC
P.O Box 6561
Albany, NY 12206
Printed in the United States of America

Copyright © 2016
ClydeBank Media LLC
www.clydebankmedia.com
All Rights Reserved

ISBN-13 : 978-1-945051-08-1

contents

Terms displayed in **_bold italic_** can be found
defined in the glossary, starting on page 95.
&
Feel free to take notes beginning on page 100.

introduction

The ITSM movement is a continual effort to reconcile the complexity of technology with the classic needs of business. To understand the need for **ITSM** (Information Technology Service Management) you must first understand the digital age in its adolescence.

"Some things never change ... and some things do."
— Captain Niobe, *The Matrix*

Technology has become so multifaceted, so complex, and so insular that it threatens the communication channels between IT and business. In today's digital-centric economy, a business's ability to effectively and seamlessly integrate its IT department with its service needs makes the difference between success and failure. Businesses will always be based on the idea of delivering a product or service that a customer needs. The essential mechanisms and tools that a business uses to accomplish these ends continually change over time to become more powerful, and potentially more complex and cumbersome. ITSM is the process of ensuring that a business's capacity to utilize technology is not dwarfed by the capacity and complexity of the technology itself.

A useful ITSM tool provides a wonderful return on investment. However, this is not a one-size-fits-all product. What's good for that little mom-and-pop company with two dozen employees doesn't necessarily fit the needs of the big corporation around the corner. So how do you find what you require? How can you determine your key ITSM tool integrations? What about a maturity assessment? Do you need to do one of those first? And what kind of other due diligence must you perform (reading product reviews, talking to vendor references, participating in demos) to find what's right for you?

Reading this book is a good start. The chapters that follow provide an in-depth look at ITIL and some of the other fundamental methodologies that have yielded successful results for businesses and their IT departments. This book also explores and analyzes real-life examples of ITSM in action. At a fundamental level, this book educates the reader on the roles of the current major concepts in ITSM. The Glossary of Terms is also a good resource for those seeking a greater command over the emerging language of ITSM methodology.

| 1 |

Technology vs. Process

Think about the potential ramifications when IT can't adequately communicate with a business. Here are a few real-world scenarios:

Mrs. Jones, a math and science teacher at a junior high school, started using a web-based teaching utility that allows for fast grading and an easier way to track assignments. The utility also provides an ample supply of practice problems that can be reviewed in the classroom. The practice problems include built-in animations that have proved incredibly helpful in aiding the students to understand the material.

The only problem with this web-based utility is that it's costing the school a subscription fee of $2500 a year, and the school principal has only recently been made aware of this steep price tag at an annual budget meeting. Upon further inquiry, the principal discovers that no teachers other than Mrs. Jones are using the utility. She has no choice but to cancel the subscription. This seems like a tremendous disservice to Mrs. Jones, one of the school's best math teachers.

While the above scenario may seem to be simply a communication problem—and it is—it is also very much a technology problem. The customer (in this case, Mrs. Jones) had an expectation that was not met due to a serious misalignment of expectations and capacity. It is this very same misalignment that has wreaked havoc on so many businesses and institutions throughout the world since the dawn of the digital age. Luckily for Mrs. Jones, she will be able to adapt and find new ways to teach algebra (even though it won't be easy), but in some situations a technological miscue resulting in a service failure can cause irreparable consequences for a business.

Here's a similar scenario to consider. A (fictitious) online book distribution company is planning for (and depends on) a massive spike in business during the holiday season. In anticipation of a larger volume of orders, the company invests in a new order processing system to boost their capacity to broker transactions and ship the products in a timely manner. Due to an ITSM failure, the new order processing system is improperly built and unable to keep up with the holiday volume. The company is forced to pay a huge amount of overtime and hire hundreds of temporary workers to process orders manually. The spike in personnel cost and the resultant loss of expected holiday net profit is staggering.

Consider the same scenario from a different vantage point. The order capacity is met, but the expense of running the system is triple or quadruple what was expected, and the IT solution itself, though effective, proves so costly that the company suffers an equally sizeable hit to its bottom line.

Focusing on Process Rather than Technology

You'll hear this notion a lot: "ITSM involves moving from a technology focus to a process focus." "Process focus" develops a language that can be shared between IT professionals, business managers, and financial managers. This language allows all parties to establish and adhere to clear expectations, progress reports, and financial strategizing. Process focus ultimately tames technology to serve the needs of business and delivers a quality result for the customer.

To understand ITSM as the natural evolution and outcome of years of problematic IT practices, we need to take a closer look at some of the IT practices that were most prevalent in the "old days" (1996–2005). The go-to IT management practices were *Network Management* and *IT Systems Management*, and each focused heavily on a collection of critical technologies that had to be learned through lengthy certification processes and were essentially Greek to anyone outside of the IT bubble.

The standard Network Management curriculum was a system of classifications, terminology, and processes that centered on a multitude of technologies. All of the ways in which IT technology was accessed under standard Network Management were extremely esoteric. Technicians used SNMP (Simple Network Management Protocol), custom XML, Windows Management Instrumentation (WMI) and a limited number of other methods. In an attempt to integrate IT with the larger business model, various schemas were in place, such as the Structure of Management Information, WBEM (Web Based Enterprise Management), the Common Information Model, and several others. These schemas posed some problems:

1. They were essentially developed for techies by techies to serve no discernible nontechnical end. It was technological organization for its own sake, without any mandate to interact with or even understand the classic, established, service-oriented needs of business.

2. Because they failed to organize around service processes, they ended up becoming highly differentiated across multiple industries. Internet service providers, for instance, focused on the development of an IT regulation system called "deep packet inspection" to attend to their common service problems, such as delays and bottlenecks in their networks. Medical tech companies were much more inclined to develop systems that didn't focus so heavily on the expedient transmission of data, but instead on safeguarding the data that was protected by the law (for example, HIPAA).

ITSM has brought the focus back to the basics of essential business operation: service. The philosophy of ITSM is powered by the belief that everything that transpires in the world of business and IT *is a service*. ITSM integrates technology with business needs and allows the handlers of IT to make decisions that make sense for the business. Concurrently, good ITSM ensures that managers are able to make key decisions with a firm understanding of their technological capacity.

One thing that both IT professionals and business managers can reasonably be expected to understand is the expectations of the customer. Consider Netflix™, for example, the internet-based entertainment network, featuring streaming movies and TV shows spanning many genres, as well as some original programming. Netflix has customers—57.4 million of them worldwide according to Forbes[1]— and those customers have certain expectations.

They expect to find a decent assortment of entertainment as a result of becoming a Netflix customer. They expect that they will be able to both browse at random and search for specific media. They expect that the media they choose to view on Netflix will be playable on their televisions, game consoles, tablets, phones, or computers without undue interruption, and that the quality of the media will be appropriate to the capacity of the device they're using to play it. Customers also expect that they will be billed for the correct amount, that their access to the Netflix service will not be interrupted, and that Netflix will keep their billing information and other personal information (such as their viewing habits) private unless they are otherwise notified. That's a lot of services for a relatively simple business model, and we've only discussed the external services due to the customer.

What about the services that need to be in place to ensure that Netflix employees get paid on time? What about the services necessary to ensure that Netflix stockholders get timely financial updates and dividends? What about the services necessary to ensure that the

---

[1] Lauren Gensler, "Netflix Soars on Subscriber Growth," *Forbes* (Jan 2015): http://www.forbes.com/sites/laurengensler/2015/01/20/netflix-soars-on-subscriber-growth/#4bc5f937409c

contracts Netflix has in place with the owners of various media are properly followed? Service demand is everywhere, and much of it depends on the skillful application of IT.

Now, let's take a look at how these service demands may be addressed through ITSM:

Fg. 1   **A Theoretical ITSM Model for Netflix**

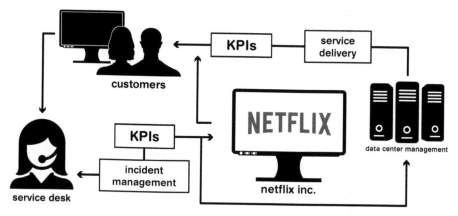

- Data center management (a defined **ITIL** process that's understood both by IT professionals and business managers) may be used to ensure that customer records, especially their billing records, are kept secure from outside intrusions, hacker attacks, and other unauthorized access.

- A **service desk** is utilized to efficiently and effectively resolve customer issues. (With 57.4 million customers, you're bound to have some problems every once in a while.)

- A system of key performance indicators (**KPIs**) is established to ensure that all of the service expectations throughout the company are being adequately met—these KPIs keep track of certain metrics, such as the average streaming quality of

Netflix media, the speed and accuracy with which payroll is processed, the average amount of time it takes a customer to log into his or her Netflix account, and any other service-oriented thresholds. Managers are responsible for monitoring these performance indicators and ensuring that they keep pace with the expectations of the company.

- Incident management (another process from ITIL) is used to dictate what happens when various systems and business modalities break down. How are incidents resolved with utmost expediency, and how is data concerning the incident captured and logged for future use?

- A system collects data about the demand for various media and the quantity and magnitude of data retrieval requests (movies being streamed) that will burden the company's service. The data collected is continually reviewed and service capacity is verified. When this is done correctly, Netflix customers are left with the expectation that, so long as they have reasonably adequate internet connections available and working devices, they can stream programming from Netflix reliably and at a reasonable quality. The end result is a positive user experience.

Good ITSM entails a seamless integration (in terms of timing and quality) of what the customer expects and what the business provides. Following are some of the key principles that are the hallmark of a strong ITSM:

- The use of highly defined processes to determine the management of IT assets

- Maintaining a strong end-point focus on the services being provided rather than the systems and technologies themselves

- The ongoing commitment to continual improvement of processes and service quality

| 2 |

ITSM & ITIL : The Difference

Not all ITSM is based in ITIL, but all ITIL is essentially ITSM. Are you adequately confused yet?

ITIL was born in the UK, technically authored by the British government, but it has since emerged to become a global standard for IT best practices. The reason ITIL is so closely associated with, and often mistaken for, ITSM is that their two respective undergirding philosophies are nearly identical—IT should efficiently and expediently address the needs of a business; service and processes, not technology, should be the focal point of effective IT. The reason that ITIL and ITSM are not the same thing is that there are a multitude of other frameworks that can contribute to ITSM besides ITIL. ITIL is just the most recognized and widely utilized ITSM standard.

Fg. 2

ITIL, as a defined process, has gone through several revisions. The most recent revision was published in July of 2011 and is commonly referred to as "the 2011 Edition." The version before 2011 was known as ITIL version 3 or "v3" (published in 2007), and before that was ITIL v2 (published in 2001). ITIL v3 introduced the notion of service as the principal focal point of the ITIL framework. Prior versions were driven more by process and split their focus into two groups: service support and service delivery. The later editions of ITIL have expanded service definitions and thus permitted a more focused approach to the maintenance and improvement of IT service functions within a business.

With ITIL version 3, the two groups were expanded into five: service strategy, service design, service transition, service operation, and continual service improvement. These five groups contribute to a developmental process commonly referred to as the "IT Life Cycle," or sometimes the "ITIL Life Cycle" or "Service Life Cycle."

Fg. 3

The ITIL Service Lifecycle

Each of the five groups contains an expandable body of *processes* and *subprocesses*, which we will list here but not define in extensive depth, since this is not an ITIL book but an ITSM book. This chapter instead provides a general overview of the five basic ITIL processes that are in use today. If you're interested in a more in-depth guide to ITIL,

ClydeBank Media's *ITIL for Beginners*[2] is a good reading selection. If you're an IT professional, or looking to develop a career as an IT professional, then you also may want to consider pursuing certification in any one (or more) of the five basic ***ITIL Life Cycle Stages***.[3]

ITIL Life Cycle Phase #1 : Service Strategy

Service Strategy commences the IT service life cycle. Though IT departments often neglect this step, it is in fact one of the most important steps in the ITIL framework and highly emblematic of its core philosophy. The Service Strategy process, rather than a lot of hands-on technical work, involves plenty of front-end planning. And, as is the case in many other facets of business, it's very easy to let the planning take the back burner while you focus instead on matters that seem more pressing, such as the daily operations of the business, putting out proverbial fires, and making sales. In ITIL the correlating processes that seem to take all the oxygen out of the room are the Service Transition and the Service Operation processes.

In true adherence to the philosophy behind both ITIL and ITSM, the Service Strategy process should be taken very seriously. It should be used as a time to fully clarify the service needs of the business alongside the realistically defined capacity of the IT infrastructure. Service Strategy is the all-important first step on a long road of cooperation that must exist between IT and the needs of the business. In addition to defining service priorities alongside service capacity, the Service Strategy process also identifies potential threats to the effective delivery of requisite services. It also gives the business a chance to focus on the "whys" rather than the "hows." IT departments tend to devote too little time to front-end strategy, and the IT professionals get sucked into the nuts and bolts of a project before the project as a whole has been

---

[2] ITIL for Beginners (Albany, NY: ClydeBank Media LLC, 2015).

[3] See *www.axelos.com* for more details on available certifications.

adequately scrutinized in light of the business's strategic requirements and financial capability.

The processes under ITIL's Service Strategy umbrella include the following:

Strategy Management for IT services

This particular process is sometimes a point of confusion, as it is alternatively referred to as both "Strategy Management for IT Services" and "Information Technology Service Management," aka ITSM. To keep the distinction intact, it's best to refer to this process using the former title. ITSM certainly encompasses a whole lot more than a single ITIL process. In terms of ITIL, this process focuses mostly on assessing the market and how the business plans to service it. ITSM, within the context of this book, is a much broader concept.

Service Portfolio Management

As the name implies, Service Portfolio Management refers to the structured analysis of various services that a business wants to offer, with a goal of determining how much they cost to deploy and the value they're bringing back to the business.

Demand Management

This process is devoted to scaling resources to demand. Demand Management requires a clear definition of the business service being provided and the costs associated with failing to meet an anticipated demand.

Business Relationship Management

This process was added in the latest 2011 edition of ITIL. Business Relationship Management focuses on identifying customers and understanding their expectations. Why the addition? As you may have noticed, somewhere near the middle of the previous decade, 2005 or so, the business world (and IT world) really went survey-crazy. Businesses have realized that obtaining useful customer feedback can be done fairly cheaply and yield powerful results. One of the implications of detailed and copious customer feedback is an enhanced ability to develop an excellent Service Strategy. ITIL's Business Relationship Management Process details the creation and operation of customer feedback registries, surveys, and complaint logs.

ITIL Life Cycle Phase #2 : Service Design

If Service Strategy is a statement of need, then Service Design is a statement of intention. In this process, the ideas discussed during the Service Strategy phase begin to take form. The end result of the Service Design life cycle phase is a proposed IT solution that's very much fitted to the determined business objective. When the Service Design phase is neglected, the business risks investing significant sums of money and manpower toward developing a subpar IT solution, or, at best, one that fails to directly address the business's needs.

Attention to the Service Design phase of the IT life cycle saves the business significant sums of money, because it's much less expensive to devote extra time to planning for a major IT rollout than to repair a botched rollout during the Service Transition or Service Operation phase.

Service Design is best considered using a wide lens, taking into account all of the various parties that will be involved in the implementation of the service, both internal and external. It's impossible for Netflix, for example, to have a Service Design that does not include current web browsers, applications, and hardware. The successful delivery of the Netflix service is just as dependent on these external service providers as it is on its own internal resources.

The solutions put forth during the Service Design phase of the IT life cycle must be financially feasible and meet the service needs of the business. Service Design solutions that are overly technical and without real service function should be discouraged. The main processes of the Service Design lifecycle phase include the following:

Design Coordination

Design Coordination involves taking stock of a Service Design's necessary component parts and ensuring that all personnel, tech, and data needed to execute the proposed design are on hand or easily accessible.

Service Catalog Management

This particular process is of the utmost importance to the Service Design life cycle phase. When a Service Design is being instituted in the Service Transition and Service Operation life cycle phases, many existing service processes are inevitably affected. Since various processes are dependent on and influence one another, it's very important that an up-to-date record (catalog) of existing IT services is maintained and accessible. Effective management of the Service Catalog reveals when and how various Service Designs will impact other existing services. These interactions must be planned for and incorporated into the overall Service Design phase of the IT life cycle.

Service Level Management

This process ensures that the business remains aware of any commitments, contracts, or other obligations.

Risk Management

This process involves taking the time to plot risk against reward. Risk is determined by the costs incurred in order to implement a potential solution, the opportunity cost of any resources that will need to be diverted, and the business risk or "business impact" of any service failures.

Capacity Management

Capacity Management involves scaling IT resources against the proposed service design. One attribute that contributes to the skill level and value of the IT professional is the ability to measure the business's technological capacity and to determine the extent of the technological assets required to perform a given task. The Capacity Management Process is there to give the IT department and business managers a chance to analyze capacity requirements with respect to real business need, as defined by the service to be delivered.

Availability Management

Availability Management complements Capacity Management by focusing on the qualitative, rather than the quantitative, capacity of an IT team to deliver a desired result. Whereas Capacity Management is concerned with quantifiable metrics such as speed, bandwidth, and service space, the Availability Management Process is focused on whether an IT department is outfitted with the requisite personnel, tools, and infrastructure to complete the project.

IT Service Continuity Management

Also commonly referred to as ITSCM, this process is concerned with the ability of the service to consistently meet all requirements to which it has contractually agreed. If a Netflix customer is paying a monthly fee for access to the Netflix media library, for example, there is an expectation that the media will continually be accessible to the customer. ITSCM assures that interruptions are contained and minimized, especially when there are contracts and service agreements in place that acknowledge a business's obligation to provide a particular service. This process operates as a kind of IT disaster response task force.

Information Security Management

Most IT service providers are entrusted with the care of private information such as email addresses, bank account info, bio-medical data, passwords, and credit card numbers. The Information Security Management Process is the part of Service Design that drills down hard on the problem of safeguarding sensitive data. This process was recently integrated into the Service Design life cycle phase with the advent of ITIL v3. In ITIL v2, Security Management was treated as a stand-alone issue. The goal of ITIL v3 was to integrate security management throughout multiple life cycle phases, beginning with the Service Design phase.

Compliance Management

Compliance Management is the legal dimension of the Service Design life cycle phase. In this Service Design process, all of the relevant internal and external regulations—from company policy to state and federal law—are reviewed, and compliance is incorporated into the design of the service. To return to our trusty Netflix example—good compliance management is needed to ensure that all streaming access to media on Netflix servers is only made available to Netflix customers with explicit authorization from the copyright holders, and that opportunities for unauthorized downloading are averted.

Architecture Management

Architecture Management focuses on the technology available to the business and the technology that will become available to the business in the future. This process is often overlooked in ITIL, as it is one of the more technology-centric processes, and ITIL's overarching concern is business-centric, with technological integration.

Supplier Management

This process ensures that the business's external suppliers of IT resources are prepared to meet the demands of the proposed Service Design. For businesses that rely, for example, on additional hosting or bandwidth procured through an outside party, the Supplier Management Process is used to ensure that the business's partners are capable. ITIL also recommends the maintenance of a separate database to keep track of suppliers and their obligations. ITIL v3 refers to this database as the Supplier and Contract Database (SCD).

ITIL Life Cycle Phase #3 : Service Transition

The Service Transition life cycle phase is the first phase in which real action is taken to implement the proposed service. This life cycle phase includes the Change Management Process, which is one of the most widely known and applied processes in all of ITIL. Service Transition is where the rubber meets the road, because it's the point at which both a business's systems and its people are forced to adapt to and learn how to use a new service delivery system. Service Transition involves either establishing a new system or revising an existing one. Especially in the latter case, risks include interruptions to service, data security breaches, and human error. Nonetheless, being able to navigate an effective Service Transition is vital to a business's flexibility and, ultimately, its survival. The ideal Service Transition is as seamless as possible for the service recipients and ultimately results in a service of superior quality and value to the business. The main processes of the Service Transition life cycle phase include the following:

Change Management
One of the most heavily utilized and discussed of ITIL's processes, Change Management implements a new IT service while minimizing the disruptions to existing services.

Change Evaluation
The Change Evaluation Process is much like a built-in Service Design phase, focused on the parameters of a specific service change. Change Evaluation is often used multiple times during the course of new service implementation (Service Transition).

Transition Planning & Support
This process is alternately referred to as "Project Management," because it is essentially just that. A multitude of project management activities are present in this process, including project planning and project reporting. Actors in this process must balance available resources with budgetary constraints and service objectives.

Application Development & Customization
The Application Development and Customization Process is devoted to building and revising applications that aid service objectives. Applications may either be developed by the business internally or be obtained through an outside vendor. ITIL doesn't dictate in any detail the nuts and bolts of developing applications. Instead, this process focuses on some of the basic interfaces that applications use to interface with the larger IT apparatus and the ITIL framework.

Release & Deployment Management

This process governs the schedule for a release with the intention of minimizing disruptions to existing services, while establishing the new service effectively and in a timely manner. Release and Deployment Management often relies on limited testing to drill down on the best method for a new rollout. The process is also used to inform and educate personnel who will be affected.

Service & Validation Testing

As the name implies, the Service and Validation Testing Process ensures that the service that results from the Service Transition life cycle phase fulfills the service needs as they were originally intended. This process is also designed to ensure that there are adequate IT resources on hand to provide this service at a high quality level on a continual basis.

Service Asset & Configuration Management

This process ensures that the IT assets necessary to deliver the service are accessible, effectively deployed, and sustainable. In order to ensure the ongoing availability of properly coordinated assets, a Configuration Management System is used to define the necessary asset interrelationships required for ongoing service delivery.

Knowledge Management

The Knowledge Management Process captures, organizes, and stores data from several processes in the Service Transition and other life cycle phases. This data is kept in the Service Knowledge Management System for future use. The main purpose of this process is to prevent wasting time and resources on recovering knowledge after it's already been obtained.

ITIL Life Cycle Phase #4 : Service Operation

Service Operation is the regular, recurring, day-to-day business of service delivery and all that it entails. The main hallmark of effective Service Operation are the reliable and repeatable delivery of expected services to the customer. A successful Service Operation life cycle phase provides working practices that ensure the regular delivery of a service. It includes a body of substantial contingency plans to address anomalies, errors, and disruptions to service norms. Service Operation also contributes to the refinement of the life cycle phases that come before it, ideally enhancing the business's capacity for Service Transition, Service Design, and Service Strategy. The following are the main processes of Service Operation:

Event Management

The Event Management Process monitors and sets classification standards for "events," or changes in the state of a system that affect the system's configuration and may prompt action from IT personnel. A structure is also instituted that analyzes trends and patterns and suggests action steps.

Incident Management

The Incident Management Process is dedicated to restoration of services in the event of an interruption. A multitude of subprocesses support the Incident Management Process in order to handle appropriate analysis of incidents and escalation steps. The subprocesses also include provisions for the closure of incidents.

Request Fulfillment

Distinct from Incident Management, the Request Fulfillment Process responds to relatively innocuous requests from service users/customers, such as password resets and basic support. An interface between Request Fulfillment and Incident Management escalates requests that turn out to be incidents.

Access Management

Access Management verifies the identity and credentials of the users of a service, ensuring that they hold the proper authorizations. The Access Management Process was added in ITIL v3 in an effort to expand security protocols into other ITIL processes. For example, Access Management interfaces with the Request Fulfillment Process to ensure that parties requesting information (such as a password change) are authorized to do so.

Problem Management

This process is essentially damage control. When an incident creates problems for the delivery of a service, the Problem Management Process minimizes damage and facilitates expedient resolution. The Problem Management Process also employs methods to identify, classify, and prioritize problems as they arise.

IT Operations Control

IT Operations Control is formally an administrative function and not a process. This function is responsible for job and routine maintenance scheduling to ensure that a service continues to be deliverable. IT Operations Control monitors infrastructure and supports basic day-by-day tasks. ITIL is careful to specifically define or prescribe all the responsibilities of the IT Operations Control function, but it does recognize that this administrative layer must be present in order for everything to work together optimally.

IT Facilities Management

Like IT Operations Control, IT Facilities Management is not considered by ITIL to be a process, but a function. As such, IT

Facilities Management is responsible for overseeing the maintenance and upkeep of the IT equipment. It is responsible for ensuring that facilities storing equipment are not open to the public but only to authorized parties. It is responsible for ensuring that IT equipment is not damaged by extreme temperatures.

ITIL Application Management

This is the operational leg of the Application Development Process from the Service Transition life cycle phase. ITIL Application Management oversees the use of applications in the delivery and improvement of IT services. It is also responsible for ensuring that personnel are trained to develop and work with necessary applications.

ITIL Technical Management

The last of ITIL's four formal functions, ITIL Technical Management simply refers to having the right personnel and technology in place to support an IT service and its underlying infrastructure.

ITIL Life Cycle Phase #5 : Continual Service Improvement

Also referred to as CSI, Continual Service Improvement evaluates and improves all other life cycle phases. Continual Service Improvement was introduced in ITIL v3 to provide a perpetual Kaizen-like feedback loop that continually sharpens the quality of the services being delivered. The essentials of CSI are gathering information, extracting value from the information in the form of lessons learned, and incorporating this knowledge back into the system as efficiently and effectively as possible. This life cycle phase has the following processes defined in ITIL:

Service Review

The Service Review Process is the reason you are continually bombarded with requests to complete surveys and give feedback for the products and services you purchase. The principle concern of this process is to determine whether or not the service being delivered meets the customer's expectations. This process generates a "Service Review Report," which is used to inform process improvement.

Process Evaluation

If the Service Review Process is concerned with the end result, then the Process Evaluation Process is concerned with the methodology. Some of the recurring themes of this process are continuity and benchmarking. Continuity involves maintaining an ongoing stream of incoming data about the effectiveness of ongoing service processes, noting particularly the extent to which current process execution emulates known best practices.

Definition of CSI Initiatives

This process is informed by the findings of Process Evaluation and Service Review. The data collected from these two processes is used to define CSI Initiatives aimed at improving service. Initiatives may be completely internal, meaning that they only involve the IT team and other service providers, or they may be external and require that the customers also be asked to do something differently. A contemporary example is the steady institution of credit cards with microchips. Merchants are being asked to cooperate with the initiative by investing in card readers that accommodate the more secure microchip technology.

Monitoring of CSI Initiatives

This process takes over where the previous process leaves off by defining and tracking the CSI initiatives that have been established. The Monitoring of CSI Initiatives Process may also instigate new improvement plans where needed.

Why ITIL?

You may be wondering how and why ITIL emerged as such a significant standard bearer for ITSM and why it has survived several decades and several iterations. As a framework that the government of the UK authored, utilized, and promoted, ITIL did indeed have some built-in legitimacy. Nonetheless, if there weren't some level of intrinsic value to ITIL, it certainly wouldn't have survived this long.

Because of the vast number of components involved, adopting ITIL best practices is not as simple as a snap of the fingers. You must have a significant amount of time and manpower to spend. It's also worth noting that there's a bit of hype built up around ITIL—there's a lot of money involved, with various private organizations offering ITIL certifications. You can also easily find an "ITIL consultant" to help you revamp your IT department. Although becoming certified in one or several of the life cycle phases associated with ITIL may be useful, you should also keep in mind that knowledge of the framework alone isn't going to magically solve all of your IT problems.

The bottom line is that frameworks such as ITIL can be highly useful, but given the vast variety of IT departments and their individual needs, the same framework won't always be optimal. This is why modern ITSM has come to incorporate elements from many different disciplines. The following chapters investigate how ITSM can be made more flexible by considering a variety of frameworks.

| 3 |

The Foundation of ITSM

In ITSM, the end goal is to provide a service. ITSM systems are thus better crafted when the needs of the end user (the customer) are kept front-and-center during the design and implementation of the new IT service. But before customer needs can be placed front-and-center, they must be clearly identified and, unfortunately, identifying customer needs is not a one-off endeavor but an ongoing and ever-changing pursuit.

Many companies have turned to surveys (and the companies that administer them) to ensure they stay attuned to customer demands. Other companies add CRM (customer relationship management) software to the mix, which tracks customers' consumption patterns along with the marketing efforts targeted at them.

As was previously noted, there are two specific ITIL subprocesses that are regularly used to keep customer needs in the forefront of IT awareness. They are "incident management" and "capacity management." The incident management subprocess, as the name implies, is used to log and resolve service issues. *Incidents* are often initiated by the customer and are not closed until the customer has been serviced with some kind of a final resolution. The ability of the customer to clearly articulate or otherwise specify the nature of the problem is critical to successful incident management.

Customers inform the capacity management subprocess by reporting their current and anticipated future service requirements. Without adequate customer involvement in capacity management, IT service providers will be forced to use guesswork when scaling resources.

The acquiring of regular and meaningful customer participation often provides widespread value to the business, beyond just IT concerns, so if you're in a position where you have to lobby your organization to invest in customer feedback, then you should find a lot of willing allies with whom you can cross-benefit.

Note : If your IT department directly drives revenue, then your most persuasive approach usually lies in the argument that more customer feedback equals more revenue opportunities.

Internal Customers

Mark Smalley of Smalley. IT points out how many businesses such as Airbnb, Uber, and OpenTable not only solicit feedback from their customers but rate their customers on a systematic basis as well. Smalley makes an interesting argument, claiming that customers should, in fact, seek out feedback from service providers and ask questions like: "How easy was it to provide me with service?" and "Was I proactive in mentioning my concerns during the service act?" Smalley contends that customers who perform favorably, so to speak, are more likely to receive better service and to realize better overall outcomes.[4]

Mr. Smalley's interesting take on two-way feedback may seem slightly off-the-wall or, at best, esoteric, but there's something of the mainstream to be learned here. In many situations ITSM efforts are used to provide services for an internal customer. Take, for example, a server at a steak restaurant who's responsible for checking for near-empty salt and pepper shakers and steak sauce bottles at the end of his shift. His assessment is presumably relayed to the restaurant's manager (the server's internal customer) who will then obtain new resources based on the information he receives.

Returning to our Netflix example, it stands to reason that there is some IT sub-entity that's responsible for collecting and compiling

---

[4] Mark Smalley, "Are You a Good Customer?" All Things ITSM (March 2016): http://allthingsitsm.com/the-provider-satisfaction-survey/

large-scale demographic data on customer viewing habits. Which type of consumers watch which kind of content? For how long? How frequently? Just as with the server's report to his restaurant manager, this demographic-based viewing information is sent to an internal customer. Smalley would likely argue that not only should the service provider's effectiveness be evaluated by internal customers, but that the internal customer should in turn be evaluated by the service provider. How clear is the restaurant manager (or Netflix business manager) about the type of data that's most useful to him? How confident is the service provider that the data he's delivering is being put to good use and that he's not wasting time and resources on an obsolete task? When the service requirements change, how well does the internal customer communicate the new needs of the business?

Good service management requires good customer management, and all efforts should be made to keep the service provider and customer on the same page at all times. In other words, when new services are being designed and implemented, be proactive and try to involve your customers at each step.

I 4 I

ITIL & Beyond

If you understand a wide range of ITSM methodologies, then you'll be more flexible and knowledgeable overall while maintaining your ITSM framework. Six Sigma, ISO 20000, and Project and Portfolio Management all offer unique views on IT success. While there's certainly no denying that ITIL is a powerful, well-known, and widely utilized framework—with a track record of positive results, some of which will be showcased in the case studies later in this book—you should be open to ways in which other ITSM methodologies can be used in lieu of or as a complement to ITIL.

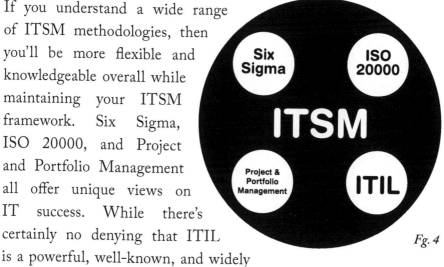

Fg. 4

Six Sigma

Like ITIL, Six Sigma was developed in the 1980s, though it is more American than British in origin. Large and small businesses alike have applied Six Sigma methodology with great success, often in conjunction with ITIL. Like ITIL v3's Continual Service Improvement life cycle phase, Six Sigma is very much geared toward effectively collecting and applying data-driven feedback. Six Sigma tends to operate at a faster pace than ITIL when it comes to measuring and producing results.

While ITIL, in all its robustness and depth, is ideal for getting a process up and running and consistently followed, Six Sigma is optimal for clearing out defects. Six Sigma uses the acronym DMAIC to define its operations, which stands for Define, Measure, Analyze, Improve, and Control. Much like ITIL, it has numerous, heavily-specific processes that underpin each of its five defined life cycle phases (Service Strategy, Service Design, Service Transition, Service Operation, and Continual Service Improvement). Six Sigma uses a system of objectives and techniques that are hierarchically defined underneath the DMAIC umbrella.

The unique synergy between Six Sigma and modern ITSM likely exists because Six Sigma is a product of the business world; it was utilized for general business long before it was applied to IT. And, given ITSM's drive to integrate IT with business needs, it only makes sense that Six Sigma would prove a valuable supplement to frameworks like ITIL, which have their roots directly in IT rather than in business.

ISO/IEC 20000

Unlike ITIL, *ISO 20000* is an audit-able framework, prescriptive rather than descriptive. ITIL, conversely, is a descriptive body of best practices, not a formal standard that's set up with strict enforcement in mind. As a prescriptive framework, ISO 20000 allows for strict verification processes. Such processes prove to be ideal for larger companies that manage multiple IT operations across the country or the globe and want to ensure that they adhere to rudimentary standards.

Remember, ITIL is an amassment of information, and IT departments aren't expected to adopt every element of ITIL. They're free instead to pick and choose. Individual IT practitioners become certified in ITIL, whereas with ISO 20000, it is the IT department at large that either obtains or fails to obtain certification.

ISO 20000 was developed in 2005 and, like ITIL, was most recently revised in 2011. Though ISO 20000 was originally developed to specifically support ITIL (along with the Microsoft Operations Framework), it can be utilized alongside other ITSM frameworks as well. ISO 20000 focuses more on the technical aspects of ITSM and thus lends itself more to explicit auditability.

ISO 20000 incorporates Support and Service Delivery Processes from ITIL and adds three other original processes: business relationship management, supplier management, and information security management. One of the factors that draws IT experts and CIOs to ISO 20000 is the relatively more concise body of standards. The most recent (2011) incarnation of ISO 20000 is only thirty-four pages long. Contrast that with the veritable library—five thick volumes—that is ITIL. You'll also notice a different tone of voice in the literature of ISO 20000. It is much more tech-friendly than ITIL, and tech-savvy readers certainly appreciate that.

Project & Portfolio Management (PPM)

Project Portfolio Management is a very broad model and not necessarily always technical. Its essential concern is the efficacy of project managers and project management offices. PPM assesses the risks and rewards of proposed projects, the financial impacts, and the importance of the desired outcomes.

A spectator sport of sorts, PPM is usually conducted from a ringside seat. The executive decision-makers leverage the process in order to determine which projects warrant a green light and which ones don't. There are essentially three big-bucket categories of analysis engaged during PPM. The first category involves careful scrutiny of the proposed project's alignment with the business's current interest. If the project does not meet the criteria, then it is not pursued. You may already be seeing the potential for interaction with ITIL here, as ITIL is devoted to aligning the energy of IT with the objectives of business.

The second point of analysis undertaken during PPM is a careful consideration of the potential interrelationships and interdependencies that may exist between various projects. The role of PPM is to use these prospective interrelationships to define how the projects will be funded, in what order, and at what priority level. The final role of PPM is monitoring the projects in progress. Often, if a project is interfering with other projects or proving to be more trouble than it's worth, it will be postponed, cancelled, or defunded. Monitoring ensures that everything goes according to plan and that any new variables that pop up are promptly addressed.

As we saw in our walk-through of ITIL, the rollout of any given service, when done well, can have a whole lot of moving parts and require much attention to detail. PPM offers IT departments an effective system by which these projects (service implementations) can be prioritized. Essentially what ITIL does, when partnered with PPM, is use "service" in lieu of "project." ITIL uses PPM to prioritize service, to aid in the decision-making process.

Note : There are a multitude of concepts in PPM, Six Sigma, and ISO 20000 that are slightly beyond the scope of this text. Rather than a full top-to-bottom survey of every dimension of these frameworks, this section focuses just on specific interaction points between these frameworks and ITSM. ITIL is unique in that it is ITSM-relevant throughout, and, since it's not as prescriptive as ISO 20000, it can be explained in relatively straightforward terminology.

Business Process Framework (eTOM)

The *Business Process Framework* is used in the telecom and entertainment industries. Originating in 1988 with the founding of the TM (TeleManagement) forum, the goal of eTOM was to create "interoperable network management products." TOM stands for the Telecom Operation Map, and its original intent, among others, was to create an enterprise-independent terminology that could be used for service management. The "e" in eTOM stands for "enhanced" and was added during a revision of the framework in 2001. Several subsequent versions of the framework have been published, and the fourteenth and latest (at print time) was issued in May of 2014.

One of the most important features of the Business Process Framework is the creation of a specific share language that can be used across several different departments, external partners, clients, and suppliers. Allowing IT enterprises to communicate more effectively lowers the risk of a misunderstanding creating a costly error, and it also makes it easier for different enterprises to come together and advance creative, effective solutions. With the framework in place and widely followed, each enterprise suddenly finds itself with more opportunities for new, valuable partnerships. Another feature of continued use of the Business Process Framework is that once specific business processes are developed, they can be cataloged for efficient reuse. The idea of reuse, not wasting energy trying to come up with new ways to solve a problem once it's already been solved, comes up again and again in the eTOM literature.

The processes of the Business Process Framework can be linked to ITIL to produce solutions that lower capital expenditure, reduce operating costs, and make integrations between technologies a lot simpler. The Business Process Framework actually contains a defined mechanism describing how to use ITIL-aligned services within the context of its own framework. The two models are disparate in certain ways and similar in others. eTOM, unlike ITIL, is a process framework, whereas ITIL is a guidance framework. Both frameworks focus on the notion of "service," each having heavy business implications.

COBIT

COBIT was created in 1996 by the nonprofit IT advocacy group Information Systems Audit and Control Association (ISACA). COBIT, as an acronym, has been referred to as Control Objectives for IT and Control Objectives for Information and Related Technology.

As a framework, COBIT defines multiple processes in terms of process inputs, outputs, key process activities, process objectives, and performance measures, combined with a rudimentary *maturity model*, which is used to steadily optimize all processes.

One of the key distinctive features of COBIT is its focus on the notion of *IT governance*, which refers to the effective and efficient application of IT to achieve the goals of an organization. COBIT is interoperable with ITIL. COBIT is more of a broad framework, dedicated to guiding an IT department to exert a level of governance that will accomplish business objectives.

There are five essential principles that COBIT follows—the principles clarify the end objectives of the COBIT strategy:

- Meeting the needs of stakeholders
- Covering the enterprise end to end
- Leveraging an integrated framework
- Cultivating a holistic approach
- Distinguishing management from governance

COBIT also makes use of seven "enablers," tools that help bring the COBIT principles to fruition:

- Principles, Policies, and Frameworks
- Processes
- Organizational Structures
- Culture, Ethics, and Behavior
- Information
- Services, Infrastructure, and Applications
- People, Skills, and Competencies

When comparing COBIT and ITIL, COBIT is thought to be more direct and is the preferred framework for IT professionals who value quick, to-the-point problem solving. ITIL is more cumbersome but has a better focus on the service aspect of ITSM. COBIT, according to some IT professionals, is more clearly benchmarked and easier to use in the context of IT auditing. COBIT also can be seen as more credible because it is authored and maintained by ISACA rather than by for-profit enterprises.

IT guru Rob England makes the argument that the authenticity and directness of COBIT, as well as the fact that it is more novel than ITIL, poises COBIT to take the reins away from ITIL as the IT standard of choice. In his argument, England implies that the underlying philosophy of ITIL encourages that blame be bestowed upon IT departments for failing to be sensitive to business needs. He cites the advent of SaaS (Software as a Service) and cloud computing as a reason why it now behooves businesses to be sensitive to the needs of their IT departments. England argues that "Organisations have failed their IT like a bad parent, and the road to redemption is via better enterprise-level governance of IT, and that's what COBIT 5 is all about."[5]

---

[5] Rob England, "Why COBIT wins in a showdown with ITIL," *The IT Skeptic* (May 2012): http://www.itskeptic.org/content/why-cobit-wins-showdown-itil

The Mechanics of ITIL Integration

With the advent of ITIL v3, ITIL now encompasses a great deal, ITIL encompasses a great deal of breadth, and its certifications subsequently offer a broad range of theoretical knowledge. But what about depth? How do IT practitioners really use ITIL to solve problems? Some in the community, such as Rob England, claim that a new, more applicable, less "chatty" framework will soon replace ITIL as the gold standard of ITSM. But the literature regarding the simultaneous use of ITIL and other ITSM frameworks shows that ITIL acts as a kind of Supreme Court, more judicial than executive in effect. A person working in the telecom industry, for instance, would be inclined to use the industry-specific protocol, eTOM, but if a conflict emerged during the course of the work, he'd be able to turn to the ITIL literature (or an ITIL-certified IT professional) to have his case "adjudicated," so to speak. Since ITIL is thought of as a descriptive methodology rather than a prescriptive one, this judicial analogy proves to be a good fit.

Fg. 5

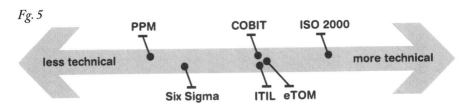

Other Ways in Which ITIL Can Be Integrated with Other Frameworks

Within the very text of ITIL there's a passage that advocates seeking opportunities to leverage other frameworks. Here's a quick recap of how and why ITIL might prove most optimal when integrated with other frameworks.

ITIL & COBIT

This framework really integrates well when there's a need for attention to management detail. The COBIT framework is a well-respected authority on the issue of differentiating IT leadership into management duties and governance, all while aggressively serving the organization's business interests. COBIT is also a great framework for incorporating a higher level of risk awareness into your IT team. COBIT provides a lens for assessing the implications of data breaches and scaling countermeasures to reduce risk. It's also worth noting that COBIT trainers are required to undergo a standardized certification process in order to teach COBIT. IT blogger Rob England draws a very interesting analogy regarding the partnership capacity between COBIT and ITIL. He compares COBIT to the CEO or general of the IT operation and names ITIL the "deep-thinking lieutenant" who offers advice but is not as prone to executive action.[6] What might we conclude from England's analogy? Perhaps that when the two are working together and in sync they are highly effective.

ITIL & eTOM

eTOM and ITIL have historically integrated well. The specialized nature of eTOM makes a non-factor for many IT professionals, but for those in the telecommunications industry, eTOM can be invaluable.

ITIL & ISO/IEC 20000

This framework lends itself well to rigorous and thorough examination. If you're just beginning to think about applying the principles of ITSM, then stick with the ITIL for a while.

---

[6] Rob England, December 5, 2014 (4:13 AM), comment on Stuart Rance, "ITIL or COBIT or something else? Which should organizations choose?," Fresh Service (blog), November 25, 2014, http://blog.freshservice.com/itil-cobit

Once you spend enough time exploring ITIL's descriptive best practices, you'll be ready to subject your IT department to the hardline, tick-mark scrutiny of ISO/IEC 20000.

Stuart Rance, a service consultant for Optimal Service Management Ltd in the UK, warns against relying too heavily on just one ITSM framework. He argues that the organization will fare better when it has some familiarity with a multitude of available frameworks and then lets its particular needs drive implementation. Rance claims that focusing too heavily on one framework to the exclusion of others will precipitate bureaucratic leadership that will soon grow tone-deaf to the realities on the ground.[7]

Mr. Rance's opinion is interesting because to some extent it runs counter to a lot of conventional wisdom floating around the IT space and other business spaces—that you should establish a leading IT framework and perhaps supplement it as needed with other frameworks. In other words, I may use COBIT to help me bolster my IT governance, but if I'm using ITIL as my principal framework, I'm not going to be nearly as well versed in COBIT as I am in ITIL. As IT blogger Rob England puts it: "I think an organization still needs a primary/lead/default framework they base their thinking on, and extend it with other bodies of knowledge as necessary." England goes on to identify COBIT as his principal "primary" framework of choice. He also proceeds to disclose his interest in the matter as a COBIT consultant.

Another IT thinker and writer, Jarod Greene, argues that the first step any IT operation should take is a self-assessment of its overall process maturity. Maturity assessments are available via companies like Gartner's and Axelos, which can give you a sense

---

[7] England, "ITIL or COBIT."

of how compatible your current IT operation is with ITIL or other frameworks.[8] These are the resources that Greene directs us to, but there's really no reason you can't come up with your own assessment of your IT operation, especially if you're already familiar with the particular ITSM framework you're keen on following. Here are some of the things you may want to consider:[9]

- To what extent does your IT department possess the ability to manage and judiciously allocate its resources?

- To what extent is your IT department able to assess and assure the ongoing execution of critical business services that are derived from IT?

- Are you able to discern the extent to which IT and the business at large is delivering service that meets the expectations of your customers?

- Are you able to accurately predict demand on IT resources such as security, hardware, and storage?

- How flexible are your IT and business teams? How much pushback do you anticipate when you attempt to integrate your new ITSM framework?

- Which person on your team do you most need to buy into your new ITSM framework?

---

[8] Jarod Greene, "Six Essential Tips for Selecting an ITSM Tool," Cherwell (June 2015): https://www.cherwell.com/blog/six-essential-tips-itsm-tool-selection

[9] Judith Hurwitz, Robin Bloor, Marcia Kaufman, and Fern Halper, *Service Management for Dummies* (Wiley, Kindle Ed., 2009), 114.

- Whose participation and support will encourage and inspire others?

If your operation isn't prepared to go full throttle on ITIL just yet, then maybe integrating one or two subprocesses may be the best path forward. Greene points out that ITSM tools, once selected, will usually affect all members of the ITSM team, so assessing front-end compatibility is a must.[10] We'll discuss the notion of "maturity" more in the following chapter.

---

[10] Greene, "Six Essential Tips for Selecting an ITSM Tool."

| 5 |

Applying ITSM

When applied correctly, ITSM boosts the service capacity and quality of a business and also saves significant sums of money. Consider the cases of Wachovia Bank and Barclays Global Investors, reviewed by Karen Guglielmo in a white paper publication, *Lean ITSM in Lean Times.*[11]

Wachovia was in the thick of a merger with Wells Fargo and was particularly interested in minimizing the damages that arose when confusion transpired. Using the Incident Management and Change Management processes defined in ITIL, Wachovia came up with a system to categorize and prioritize **events** as they arose. Wachovia, being a massive banking company, accepted that there would inevitably be a spike in incidents that would lead to a loss in revenue. The key would be to use available resources intelligently and resolve incidents in a well-prioritized way. Wachovia used a metric called RTO, or Return to Operation. The RTO metric contained data on how much money was being lost per minute and per second for various incidents. This event, incident, and change management approach allowed Wachovia to save about $20 million, according to Paul Ruppel, production systems consultant lead at Wachovia.

The Wachovia team chose to focus on a particular subset of ITSM, or specifically of ITIL, practices—Change Management, Event Management, and Incident Management—and achieved good results. Throughout the literature on ITIL and ITSM, these particular

---

[11] Karen Guglielmo, "Lean methodologies for lean times," TechTarget (June 2009): http://itknowledgeexchange.techtarget.com/total-cio/lean-methodologies-for-lean-times/

processes come up time and again. They are thought to be among ITIL's more "mature" processes, meaning they've been used and refined to such an extent that good results can typically be expected from using them. Wachovia's decision-makers most likely recognized the relatively high maturity of these processes before deciding to rely on them.

It behooves IT managers to consider *process maturity* when deciding how to leverage ITIL or any other ITSM tool. Specific models can be used (the *Capability Maturity Model*, or CMM, being the most common) to assess the maturity of a process. The Software Engineering Institute at Carnegie Mellon University created CMM in 1986, originally to benefit software developers. Today, it is used throughout a multitude of IT enterprises.

The CMM model emphasizes developing processes in order to reuse them. If you're going to invest a lot of time and energy in process improvement—which is all the rage these days with customer surveys, feedback implementation, and the recent focus on the Continual Service Improvement ITIL life cycle phase—then you'll need to develop processes that are repeatable and replicable across the organization. In order to enforce the repeatability of various processes, organizations mandate process repeatability in their Standard Operating Procedure guides and general policy frameworks.

Another powerful tool that the CMM model leverages is the strict definition of procedures within the company with replicability in mind. Specific IT departments are required to detail their procedures in explicit detail while making sure that they aren't so explicit that they can be usable in only one or another department. They need to be usable throughout the company to the broadest extent possible.

The CMM model also relies on the capability of an organization to measure its progress using clear quantitative metrics. Even if a process doesn't intuitively lend itself to this kind of measurement, the IT department following CMM protocol finds creative ways to measure the results and functionality levels of their processes.

The Five Levels of CMM

CMM uses five evolutionary stages, or levels, to help define the extent to which a process has reached maturity.

Level 1 : Initial

In this stage, the IT department is not doing much more than spit-balling. Ad hoc approaches are pursued using only the most general of guidelines from ITIL or other sources. The IT department may issue some policy statements regarding the purpose of the process and roughly defining the path forward, but there are at this time no formally dedicated resources and no substantial signs of commitment. Though there is a high level of creative freedom at this stage, the chances aren't very high for profitability or highly efficient service.

Level 2 : Repeatable

Repeatability is the threshold that identifies Level 2. There need not be more than just the most basic processes set up, but so long as they can be reliably repeated, they qualify as Level 2 in the process maturity hierarchy according to CMM. Level 2 maturity is, by definition, without any form of measure or control. Furthermore, the various roles and responsibilities involved in carrying out the process are vaguely defined or not defined at all.

Level 3 : Defined

When a level of documentation is introduced that truly defines a process, then Level 3 has been achieved. At Level 3, multiple repeatable processes can be integrated together into a master process. The roles and responsibilities that lacked definition in Level 2 are now clearly defined and well communicated. Quality targets have been set, as well as formal management reports.

Level 4 : Managed

In order for a process to move from Level 3 to 4, there must be more than just rudimentary documentation on the process. There must also be some system of measurement that is capable of verifying the process's efficacy. The process is thus considered to be a "managed" process, since it is subject to clearly defined standards, is documented, and is repeatable. At this level the notion of "inputs" and "outputs" can be defined and used. Inputs can be taken from other Level 4 or higher processes and used in the existing Level 4 processes. A Level 4 or higher process may also be used to generate outputs to inform other processes. By the time a process has reached Level 4, its overall quality has substantially improved over that of Level 1. And, in addition to inputs and outputs, various performance metrics have been developed and refined to a point at which they can be transferred between departments and applied to other processes for evaluation purposes.

Level 5 : Optimized

Remember the fifth ITIL life cycle phase, Continual Service Improvement? The fifth level is achieved when the process is being improved continually. Perhaps this involves exercising, in very high gear, the processes defined in ITIL's fifth book (CSI). But in order for a process to attain optimized maturity, it must have established a compelling feedback loop and maintenance routine that demonstrates a capacity for ongoing improvement. Optimized processes, because they are at the apex of maturity, are able to inform corporate policy.

Note : CMM may also refer to a level "0" meaning that there are as of yet no indications at all that a process is being developed.

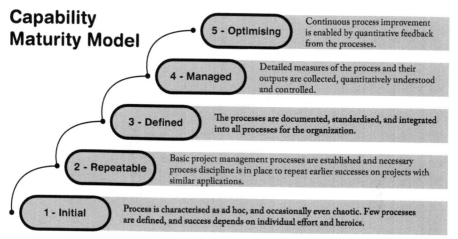

Capability Maturity Model

5 - Optimising — Continuous process improvement is enabled by quantitative feedback from the processes.

4 - Managed — Detailed measures of the process and their outputs are collected, quantitatively understood and controlled.

3 - Defined — The processes are documented, standardised, and integrated into all processes for the organization.

2 - Repeatable — Basic project management processes are established and necessary process discipline is in place to repeat earlier successes on projects with similar applications.

1 - Initial — Process is characterised as ad hoc, and occasionally even chaotic. Few processes are defined, and success depends on individual effort and heroics.

Fg. 6

The Service Catalog

When Nilesh Patel was hired as the director of infrastructure service management at Barclays Global Investors, he was tasked with creating a ***service catalog***, a utility that would show both IT and the business as a whole the available IT services alongside their costs and delivery times. Patel claimed that the true reason for developing the service catalog was to help "deepen our understanding of the drivers of IT cost," not specifically to reduce costs in any one area of the company. "We actually had a good handle on internal IT costs," Patel said.[12] The real issue was that the Barclays IT department had been growing by leaps and bounds in response to the pace of business, and the company wanted to make sure that the appropriate processes were in place to economically scale the growth of IT to the growth of the business. To make smart IT decisions, the ability to understand the dynamics of IT was a must, as was using ITIL's "everything is a service" model.

Developing mature processes and studying service catalogs don't in and of themselves create optimal IT. So much of the ITSM philosophy involves nonstatic forces, such as the continual search for process

---

[12] Guglielmo, "Lean Times."

improvement. In order for ITSM to find positive expression within a business, the business must exude a habitable culture for strong ITSM. To do this, the business must invest in the personnel and training needed to bring the core ITSM philosophies, such as those found in ITIL, to the doorstep of the business.

During the Wachovia merger with Wells Fargo, the staff was reduced in several departments and two massive pools had to be combined. This was accomplished using the *configuration management database*, which helped the newly combined and reduced IT teams figure out which processes needed to be kept and which could be discarded.

> *Note : The Configuration Management Database (CMDB) is a tool commonly used in IT departments to organize various IT assets across the organization. The CMDB keeps track not only of the identity of the department's assets, but also tracks the various relationships shared between different assets.*

The result was the management of a larger IT workload with fewer staff members, thanks to the utilization of ITIL's configuration management process.

ITSM Leadership Must Be From the Top Down

In her white paper, Karen Guglielmo emphasizes the importance of executive support for ITSM initiatives, referring to ITIL and ITSM not as projects but as "journeys."[13]

If you think about it, the argument for the necessity of sweeping cultural change is a prerequisite for success with ITSM. If you've ever been a part of any large corporate or business team, in IT or in any other field, then you know that there can be a lot of resistance to change. People gravitate toward what's simple, repetitive, and familiar. If you put a truck loader with Truck A and leave him there for several hours,

---

[13] Guglielmo, "Lean Times."

he begins to pick up on the rhythm and flow of the loading process for Truck A. Tell him you want him to move to Truck B, and you're bound to get resistance, even if the material going into Truck B is essentially the same as that going into Truck A. Telling an IT department that they need to begin following a new process, filling out different types of paperwork, and approaching problem solving in a completely different way is also inevitably going to lead to pushback.

The only way to effectively prevent pushback from stifling your ITSM changes in their tracks is to get a firm commitment from executive level management. If you're the CIO of an organization and have decided that it's in the company's best interest to implement COBIT, then you need to acquire the committed support of the company president/CEO to drive the behavior change necessary for the transition. ITSM in many important ways is a culture shift, and cultural shifts require behavioral shifts.

You may not be able to get universal adoption of ITSM throughout your organization overnight, but if you can cordon off a section of the IT apparatus that you *do* control and are able to show substantial benefit from pursuing ITSM in that area, then you will likely attract the attention of the higher-ups, making them more amenable to proliferating your ITSM methods throughout the company. Who knows? They may even appoint you to serve as an ITSM/ITIL ambassador and let you spearhead the enterprise-level changes.

Change is not easy. All it takes is one person in your IT department with a negative, skeptical view of ITIL, COBIT, or whatever you choose to implement. This type of negativity can provide a nice, convenient reason for many other team members to stay put in their cozy routines. You'll have to overcome this inertia by laying out a vision for how the changes will improve everyone's experience. Getting your team members to buy into the prospect of positive change, combined with maximum support from executive level leadership, gives you the best chance at substantial, lasting change.

With regard to getting your employees to "buy in," it's important that, as a CIO or department manager, you don't lose sight of some of the unique, ground-level insights your employees may possess. If there is substantial resistance to change toward ITSM, then you shouldn't immediately assume that your employees are simply lazy. You should instead use their insights to inform the development of your new processes and be mindful of separating baseless pouting from reasonable argument.

One highly effective way to deal with the naysayers and signal to your team that the company is serious about these changes is to invite outside experts to talk about ITIL, COBIT, or whichever ITSM system you're looking to implement. A good spokesperson should be able to adequately respond to criticism of the system while also painting a highly compelling picture of what could be accomplished through the successful implementation of the systems. For ITIL, there are several established services that offer seminars, such as Pink Elephant and Axelos. Involving outside experts can also be useful in persuading upper management—even those individuals with no explicit understanding of IT—to get behind your efforts. In addition to seminars, you can invest in specific ground-level training for your employees to show them your commitment and try to persuade them to get on board.

Another serious problem you'll come up against is the difficulty of declaring an ITSM "victory." Since you're dealing with a cultural change, there's not going to be a clear project end point at which you declare the transition accomplished. ITIL itself has a "continual improvement" phase enshrined within its core. And the principle of continual improvement runs ubiquitous throughout all of ITSM; it's always a continual work-in-progress, not a project. To accommodate this reality, you should space out and diversify your ITSM training regimens. Keep your communications on ITSM engaging, routine but not monotonous. Keep your team moving towards an ITSM culture by allowing them to continuously learn and be encouraged. Also keep executive support visible by making ITSM-inspired metrics a part of standard employee performance evaluations.

The Step-By-Step Breakdown of ITSM Implementation

Regardless of which framework you adhere to, when you're moving your IT department toward ITSM, you're going to follow a similar series of action steps.

To speak in very broad terms, you must accomplish the following:

1. You must evaluate, understand, and be able to describe in systematic terms the nature of your current IT system. Take a look at the processes and infrastructure you have in place, the services you offer, and the critical personnel.

2. You must craft a vision for an improved, service-oriented IT department. In particular, you should qualify and quantify the services that the new IT department will be able to deliver and improve upon. During this step you can define the formal frameworks and methodologies you'd like to employ, such as ITIL, Six Sigma, or COBIT.

3. You need to draft a rudimentary plan that shows a feasible way you can get from point A to point B—point A being your current IT layout and point B being your desired outcome, post changes.

4. You need to list the key steps your IT department needs to take to arrive at your sought-after destination.

As you continue to implement your ITSM framework (remember, it's an ongoing process) you need to focus your management efforts in five critical areas:

1. **The People** : We discussed earlier in this chapter the importance of a cultural buy-in from your IT personnel. Continued attention to and investment in your staff is critical for the ongoing introduction of any serious ITSM initiative.

2. **The Processes** : Having well-defined and sharp processes in place to fit the business and service needs of your organization is critical. Your processes act like laws in a way, in that you, your executive leadership, and members of the IT service team can refer to them.

3. **Technology** : Though your technology isn't the center-point of your ITSM operation (service is your center-point), your technology is a critical tool that you need to use to accomplish your IT service goals. Managing your technology—with respect to business implications, such as cost, efficiency, usability, and so forth—must be done with expert care.

4. **Organization** : Organization is distinct from "process" in that it refers to the IT department's holistic function within the business rather than to the particular processes used within the IT department. Your IT department's organizational vitality must be assessed in terms of its ability to effectively interact with executive management, other departments, and outside vendors and partners. It's also important for the departments outside of IT to understand the fundamentals of ITSM and to support and advance the ITSM culture.

5. **Integration** : For ITSM, integration is a critical evaluation point. The big-picture objective of ITSM is to align IT energy with business interest. This integration—the degree of seamlessness with which IT efforts can be translated into business goals—does much to define the success of your ITSM initiative.

In many situations, organizations stand to benefit from hiring an outside consultant that specializes in the ITSM framework being implemented. On the downside, outside consultants don't have intricate knowledge of your IT and business operations. But on the upside, outside consultants don't have intricate knowledge of your IT and business operations! No, that's not a misprint. It's an acknowledgment that sometimes having a fresh pair of eyes on your operation can prove tremendously beneficial. Routines can be blinding.

In addition to consultants, there are a wide range of classes available that train in ITSM. If you do decide to go the classroom route, however, please make sure that all of the involved parties participate in the class, not just a few. ITSM has a ubiquitous quality, in that, when it's implemented properly, it will affect every cubicle of your IT department. Having just a few of your IT staff members attend classes and relying on them to proliferate their learning throughout the rest of IT is a losing strategy.

To further enhance and speed up the learning process, be sure to stock up on the publications that are relevant to your ITSM implementation. Some of these pubs can be expensive. Remember to be realistic about the capabilities of your enterprise. Odds are you won't be going from zero to the full five ITIL service life cycle phases in a matter of weeks. Acquire the books that contain information on the processes and subprocesses on which you plan to focus in the near term. The same can be said of ITSM course offerings. The ITIL courses offered by Axelos, for example, are divided by service life cycle phase. Use the ones you need.

| 6 |
Why Strategy Is So Important

When configuring IT resources to accommodate service objectives on an ongoing, ever-changing, always on-point, and always flexible basis, you'll need to accept a certain amount of uncertainty about the future demands you may encounter. In many ways, ITSM is a lot like playing a game of chess: you're positioning your resources in places where you anticipate they'll prove useful. However, as with chess, the game board is not static and a few moves may force you to adopt a new set of tactics or perhaps a new strategy altogether.

ITSM strategy involves being aware of the range of possibilities that you could face over time and doing your best to predict and plan for these possibilities. Too many organizations fail to operate with a strategy and instead *react* their way through their ITSM needs. If service fails in one sector, they'll hurriedly throw resources at that sector to put out the fire, but will they devote time to going back to the drawing board and considering what might be done to prevent similar incidents from occurring in the future? In most businesses, sufficient devotion to strategy involves willing yourself away from the pressing concerns of the business and forcing yourself to take a longer, slightly abstract view of the business's velocity.

As tech people, strategizing can be exceptionally difficult, because we're used to operating within a clear-cut, problem–solution tactical modality. The abstractness of strategy scares us. Nevertheless, what should scare us more, ironically, is failure to strategize.

The important thing to remember here is that your ITSM strategy doesn't have to be perfect. You're not going to anticipate every future demand of your business or even of your IT department. The actual process of developing and pursuing a strategy is valuable in and of itself. Even if it turns out to be mediocre, pursuing a mediocre strategy tenaciously for three years will leave you better off than you'd have been without any strategy at all.

Where to Begin

When it comes to initiating an ITSM strategy, more participation is usually better. If possible, draft a committee to be in charge of establishing your strategy. Be sure to include members from outside the IT sphere, such as business and financial managers.

At the core of ITSM is the alignment of technology with business objectives. Therefore, your ITSM strategy should begin with a vivid assessment of business needs. You want to convert "information technology" into "business technology."

Once you have a clear understanding of the near, medium, and long term business objectives that you will be supporting, you need to decide on a system of relevant metrics that will help you chart progress and adapt when necessary. Selecting optimal metrics can prove a tricky task, and for IT people, establishing metrics is an unfortunate opportunity to fall back into the older technology-centric modes of thinking in which the needs of the business are forgotten. You don't want to get lazy here and develop metrics simply because they're convenient and easy to track on a technical level. You need metrics that are going to directly support the *business objectives* you've identified.

Don't be afraid to take a long view during your ITSM strategizing. In fact, if possible, create a strategy that can span several years. If your strategy can remain even moderately effective throughout an extensive period of time, then you won't have to worry about going back to the drawing board and reinventing your ITSM approach—you'll be able to move forward, full throttle.

The Service Management Plan

Many IT operations produce an annual plan to supplement their overall ITSM strategy. Service management plans, in the context of ITIL, are used to support the Continual Service Improvement process. One of the principle roles of the service management plan should be to strengthen the communication channels between the IT service provider and the customer. Existing methods of obtaining customer feedback should be assessed and improved where possible. The relevance of various sources of customer input should be scaled. Customer data should be made accessible to relevant parties, and metadata strategy should be reviewed and improved as needed.

As with ITSM strategy development, development of the service management plan should include the participation of many different players in the organization, such as business managers, IT managers, and frontline IT service providers.

During the formation of the service management plan, ITIL's Service Design process also comes into play, particularly the service catalog management subprocess. The service management plan should inform, update, edit, and expand the existing service catalog to reflect the immediate business requirements of the organization.

If you're having any trouble understanding the difference between the "service strategy" and the "service management plan," think of it this way:

Your IT service strategy helps you determine what it is you need your IT department to accomplish, whereas the service plan outlines specifically *how* these objectives will be accomplished. You should also realize a timeline distinction, in that the service plan should be revisited and rebooted annually, whereas the service strategy should last for several years.

Fg. 7

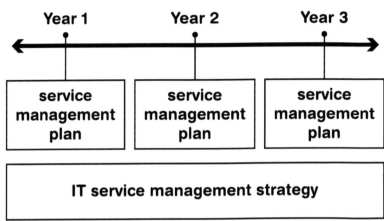

Incorporating Automation into ITSM Strategy

IT blogger Neven Zitek has an interesting story about IT service automation. The tale features an IT department that had become dismayed by their customers' inability to remember their passwords. The IT department was being regularly bombarded by requests for password resets. The task, in and of itself, was not terribly daunting, but the repetitiveness of it was enough to drive anyone mad. The IT team decided on a solution that relied on automation. Customers would now be prompted to change their passwords every month. This solution would not only better secure customer data, but it would also ensure that customers were regularly exposed to their current passwords.[14]

What makes Zitek's example particularly noteworthy is how the customers themselves were incorporated into the automated solution. Rather than try to develop some complex code that could verify identity and then reissue passwords, the IT department got ahead of the problem by having all customers recreate their passwords on an ongoing basis.

---

[14] Neven Zitek, "ITIL Service Automation – Are we even needed anymore?," *20000 Academy* (July 2014): http://advisera.com/20000academy/blog/2014/07/22/itil-service-automation-even-needed/

Automation is an important part of ITSM strategy, but it's important for IT professionals to discern what's really worth automating and how best to achieve the desired outcome. The obvious benefits of automation are the savings realized by eliminating the human labor component and the reliable accuracy achieved when a process is successfully automated. What's not always so obvious is how difficult it can be to automate certain processes in an efficient way that will result in enduring benefit. Things can change fast, and if your automation efforts aren't adequately designed to accommodate the context of your ITSM strategy, then you may end up wasting valuable time and resources on automation for a disproportionately small or nonexistent benefit.

To quote the chess master Emanuel Lasker, "When you see a good move, look for a better one." If the IT professionals in Zitek's example hadn't taken the time to consider multiple approaches to their customer password problem, they may have ended up pursuing a complicated and ultimately non-sustainable automation effort. Look for ways to automate that will weather change while providing a clear and direct benefit.

| 7 |

Beyond Theory

This chapter will review a few case studies in ITSM application, beginning with the story of an international telecom company that found out firsthand how important it is to have both sound ITSM theory and practice when attempting change.

The Tragedy & Redemption of the ITIL Dream Team

Let's call the company GlobalComm. The following account is factually based, but we don't want to give the impression that we're speaking on behalf of the company or any of its specific stakeholders. GlobalComm is a global telecommunications company with more than 6,000 employees and a revenue stream of $4 billion per year. The company was built using a strategy that emphasized growth above all else, and in growth, they were indeed quite successful. In efficiency— not so much. GlobalComm, to its credit, encouraged innovation and expansion at the local levels, giving lower level management authority to open and aggressively expand new frontiers of business and technology. This was a great philosophy for growth, but without a strong centralized management core, the IT scene ended up woefully convoluted, with differing setups everywhere and no feasible way for IT silos within the company to communicate with one another. The executive leadership, for its part, was certainly not just sitting idle while allowing the underlings to build profit. Quite the contrary. They were combing the market looking for purchase opportunities. They bought up smaller companies at quite an impressive clip. Unfortunately, however, since there was no centralized IT framework in place, the executive brass was content to just leave the existing IT infrastructures in place while they went off after their next conquest. Before long, GlobalComm was peppered with so many different IT designs, and significant opportunities for efficiency and cost reduction were being so obviously missed, that they started to be palpable on the bottom line. Redundancies were everywhere. Finally, GlobalComm took action and decided to implement ITIL.

GlobalComm was by no means late to the ITIL party. They had experimented with the framework here and there, but the problem was that the fast-paced growth of the business continually stole away all the necessary attention from ITIL implementation. ITIL had failed before it was given a chance to succeed.

The new approach was different. GlobalComm specifically recruited and hired a group of formally-certified ITIL techs (12 of them altogether) and had them report directly to executive management. GlobalComm was clearly serious about solving its IT problem. A decision was made to keep the new ITIL dream team separate from the rest of the IT personnel. They were to work together to create a dramatic plan to transform GlobalComm's IT infrastructure into one that adhered to the guidance set forth in ITIL, to the hopeful end of unifying the company's IT components and then benefitting from the advantages of teamwork and cooperation.

It took the ITIL dream team about a year to put their plan together. Over the next several months, the plan seeped down and spread throughout GlobalComm's many IT operations. The general consensus coming back regarding the plan was that it made perfect sense at a theoretical level, but was wildly impractical given the current, highly disparate state of the company's IT affairs. No one had a clear step-by-step sense of how to make use of the plan without severely disrupting the normal IT operations of the company.

Meanwhile, GlobalComm certainly didn't curb its appetite for growth, acquiring yet another company and adopting new VoIP (Voice Over Internet Protocol) technology as part of its product repertoire. The ITIL project floundered and was soon subjected to a complete redesign.

The new design was released six months later and, like the previous design, was created with almost total insulation from the ground-level IT operations. The second ITIL plan was more successful than the first. Thanks to its prescriptions, some departments were able to merge, workloads were reduced, and more efficient processes were created. But despite these gains, it was clear that GlobalComm had yet to realize the full range and depth of benefits that had been realized by other businesses that had fully implemented ITIL.

The ITIL project sat on the back burner until the company's aggressive growth practices eventually led it to bite off a bit more than it could chew in the form of a new series of customer contracts. It became apparent that in order to service the new customer contracts, GlobalComm would have to reorder its IT system in an effective way. This was GlobalComm's third attempt at successfully adopting ITIL, and this time it was agreed that the approach should be bottom-up rather than top-down. This plan wasn't created in an isolated office with no attention given to ground-level realities. Instead, a systematic intake of interviews and local analyses were pursued to get a clear reality-based view of which processes needed to be altered, how, and when, in order for ITIL to be implemented with the utmost efficacy. Meetings were scheduled with local department heads, and actionable schematics were drawn up dictating the time frames for changes. Workflows were created that actually made sense and could be acted upon. Before long, a sense of true momentum was palpable. IT departments that had never before communicated with one another were suddenly making great use of each other, transferring tech, personnel, and ideas at a level of efficiency of which they could be proud. Perhaps most critical was the establishment of a Configuration Management Database. Before long, cost-savings opportunities were actualized. Duplication of tools and labor was reduced, and GlobalComm found itself with a less costly and more agile IT department.[15]

What's to Be Learned?

In the GlobalComm case study, one of the most interesting phenomena to note is the fact that there were three separate attempts to implement ITIL before the good results began to pour in. When we assess the timeline of this story, there's a suggestion of a kind of critical mass that, once reached, will result in the new system's successful incorporation.

This critical mass occurs when enough solid ITSM procedures are being followed, enough benefits are being realized, and, most critically, enough of the personnel are beginning to buy in, yielding ever more and greater successes. Another incredibly important lesson here is that moving your IT department to an optimized ITSM framework, like ITIL, is never impossible, even if the company's aggressive growth practices over the years have left it with an utter hodge-podge of IT systems. However, if your company does decide to pursue growth first and organization second, the leadership should plan for a much more difficult, time-consuming, and costly transition into ITSM. Therefore, if a solid ITSM framework, like ITIL, is the end goal, it's better to start the wheels turning sooner rather than later.

It's also important to make the wheels turn in a way that yields the best chance at success. The GlobalComm example clearly shows that the ITIL framework is best imposed with support from the top but with practical knowledge from the ground level.

---

[15] Chris Matney, "ITIL case study: How one company turned around a bad experience," Network World (March 2006): http://www.networkworld.com/article/2309147/infrastructure-management/itil-case-study--how-one-company-turned-around-a-bad-experience.html

Finally, we can and must take away that the creation and use of a Configuration Management Database (CMDB) is critical in instituting successful ITSM in an organization. The CMDB comes up over and over again in the literature, such as in the following case study involving a real company called Finisar and its director of global IT, Christine Rose.

Making Good Use of the CMDB

"The CMDB is the core of ITIL," according to Christine Rose. "It allows you to track your assets and gives you a running history of everything you've done."[16]

The CMDB is equal parts data hub, historical center, inventory list, and technology map. A properly maintained CMDB provides a listing of all technical assets that a business owns.

Often, the CMDB can make problem solving incredibly simple. In the case of Finisar, the company's FTP server was creating a disproportionate number of incidents. This particular service was responsible for providing technical support for end users. IT was able to use the history in the CMDB to trace the recent usage volume of the server and found that it had recently been much more heavily used. The customer-facing side of the business, even though it likely experienced a higher volume of requests in its service centers, did not alert IT to watch out for an overload of their servers. Nor should they have.

Imagine a support center that has a few exceptionally busy weeks. The phones are ringing off the hooks, the emails are flying in, and everyone is generally busting his or her you know what to keep up. Perhaps the support center manager hires new team members to keep up with the growing demand. In the midst of all this activity, it's not to

---

[16] Ben Worthen, "Finisar," CIO.com (September 2005): http://www. itsmcommunity.org/downloads/Case_Study_-_Finisar.pdf

be expected that the support center manager or a member of the team is going to wonder how this recent business trend is going to affect the IT department. The service center employees are there to serve the customers, not the techies.

ITSM offers methods that can keep the IT resources accommodating the pace of business. Thanks to the CMDB, it was easy to simply add more storage space to the FTP server's hard drive. "If we did not have a history of the server, we would not have noticed the trend, since the business didn't convey its needs to IT," says Rose regarding the situation at Finisar.

In addition to making problems eminently more solvable, the CMDB can assist ITSM efforts in several ways. If there is a proposed change to an IT system, the CMDB can be consulted to determine the extent to which the change will affect other systems.

"There are a lot of things that the business does that IT just doesn't know about," says Rose. "[ITSM] allows us to align ourselves with the business instead of just making them angry when something they need isn't available." Rose's implementation of ITSM was responsible for raising customer satisfaction rates from 33 percent to 95 percent. Finisar has also been able to cut costs from 4 percent down to 2.4 percent.[17]

If you've never used a CMDB before, here's what you can expect. The CMDB is able to display hierarchical relationships between various components of the IT infrastructure. The data can be filtered, grouped, or sorted in various ways and can be marshaled into a variety of different reports.

The CMDB can be used to assign and monitor service requests and to report and process incidents. Critical KPI (key performance indicator) data can be retained from the CMDB as well.

---

[17] Worthen, "Finisar."

The CMDB can store personal records as well as technical records, and it may define the various relationships between technology and user(s). Remember, the entire point of the CMDB is to provide a tool that can be used when pursuing service management activities. When a service manager is trying to create the perfect Service Transition team, he needs to know what technology is available and who knows how to use it.

Fg. 8

The Configuration Management Database

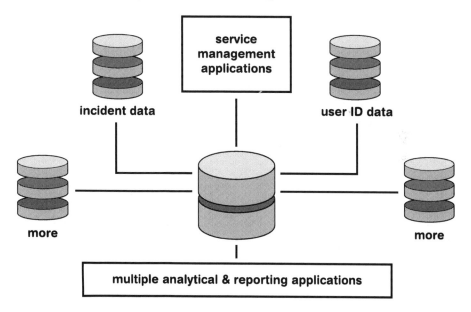

The data that interacts with a CMDB comes from many different sources and is handled by different software. It's no small feat to ensure that this data all blends well together once it hits the CMDB. A special layer of programming is used, called the *Integration Infrastructure*, to ensure that all of the data that's used by the CMDB can be integrated together in a meaningful way. A good integration infrastructure is the difference between comparing apples to oranges and apples to apples.

| 8 |

The Key Roles of ITSM

As this book has continually emphasized, ITSM is not a project, but a cultural change. As such, the role of the IT professionals is critically important. When ITSM changes are implemented in a company, it involves a whole lot more than just changing the paperwork and reporting methods and the way technology is configured. The most important change is in the way the IT professionals do their jobs. To achieve success with ITSM, IT professionals are required to adjust the way they think about and execute tasks throughout their workdays. They are required to change the ways in which they communicate with their coworkers, both inside and outside of IT. They may even be asked to change their job titles or to give up certain hierarchical relationships in certain circumstances.

> *Note : An example of giving up hierarchical status can be found in the **Scrum** methodology. Scrum is a way of managing projects using short, iterative, team-centered bursts of work. Scrum relies on "self-organizing" principles, which entail a commitment to constant forward progress via flexible and interchangeable roles. An employee can be working on a scrum project with his direct supervisor and the two can be, for all intents and purposes, equals during the course of the project.*

Each IT operation, and each ITSM methodology, may necessitate different roles. This chapter will provide a generalized view of what types of roles are needed for ITSM.

The Service Manager

The Service Manager is the boss. Kind of. He's more like the head on a long powerful snake that's composed of the service team. It falls on the Service Manager's shoulders to define particular services and how they're to be delivered in accordance with business expectations. It's quite an important interpretative role, because ITSM, for all its theoretical emphasis on aligning IT with business interests, leaves it up to the organization to define the business interests. The Service Manager is responsible for making this determination. Therefore, it's imperative that the Service Manager has an understanding of what's going on in the business beyond IT. It can be useful to appoint a Service Manager from outside the IT department, as long as he or she has the requisite technical literacy and a working knowledge of the organization's basic IT capabilities.

When ITIL is being used as the ITSM framework, it's the Service Manger's role to oversee the institution of ITIL processes. Depending on the size and ambition of the IT staff, adopting ITIL best practices can be a highly demanding task. The Service Manager must decide how ITIL guidance can best be integrated into the organization, the who, the how, and the when. Remember, ITIL is descriptive, not prescriptive. It's there to provide guidance, not to prepare you for an ITIL inspection—there's really no such thing as a formal ITIL inspection.

Note : This is not to say that businesses can't hire someone to create an inspection that involves verifying certain ITIL-recommended processes. Essentially, though, ITIL is designed to be a reference. For more audit- and inspection-friendly metrics, see ISO/IEC 20000.

Here's a common method Service Managers use to determine service needs:

First, the Service Manager answers three basic questions concerning the expectations of the customer. A good Service Manager must understand at least this much about his customer's experience.

1. What service is the customer expecting and how is it delivered?
2. How is the service used?
3. How much does the service cost?

Second, and finally, the Service Manager must answer two basic questions about the IT department's capability (and responsibility).

1. How is the service supported?
2. How is the service delivered?

A service is supported when the IT department's resources are deployed to an extent necessary to meet the demands of the customer. In the Finisar case study, the IT department was responsible for providing enough server space so the customer support team could do its work.

A service is delivered when the IT department produces a particular product or report that fulfills the customer's need. This product can be for an internal customer, such as an important financial report that's built into Oracle and derived from multiple databases, or the product can be for an external customer, such as a customizable web page design palette that anyone can use.

As this book mentioned before, the most common ITIL processes are Change Management and Incident Management.

With regard to Change Management, it is the role of the Service Manager to ensure that there is a back-out plan at the ready in case the change being implemented begins to compromise basic service. The Service Manager must also provide a clear assessment of the risk associated with any given change and is responsible for communicating the fundamental elements of the change to the Service Team and any other relevant parties.

The Service Manager's job with respect to Incident Management is very simple: restore service as quickly as possible, isolate the cause of the incident, and take action to prevent the incident from recurring.

The Service Team

Think of the Service Team as a kind of board of directors, responsible for advice and execution during the course of a service change. The Service Team's primary duty is to keep the Service Manager well informed of all relevant data, since it is the Service Manager who acts in an executive role. Service Teams are often a motley collection of tech experts, support staff, product experts, and even executive leadership.

> *Note : With regard to having executive leadership on a Service Team, there is another common ITSM position known as a Service Sponsor, which is usually occupied by a party who's directly privy to the business side of the company. This person is responsible for setting the budget for services, setting acceptable service levels, and qualifying associated risks.*

After the service is implemented, it is the Service Team's role to ensure that the service remains effective. If there are opportunities for improvement of a service, then the Service Team should be the first to make the suggestion. The Service Team is also expected to contribute to the product service catalog when appropriate.

Because Service Teams are front-and-center in service design and delivery, they're also expected to play a role in long-term planning, anticipating what the evolution of technology and business will require months and years down the road.

In conjunction with the Service Manager, the Service Team should be involved in accountability and tracking metrics to determine performance. The Service Team uses these metrics to make recommendations and determinations about service changes.

Since the Service Manager and Service Team are spearheading your ITSM efforts, their ability to work together is essential. Regular meetings are a must. You may also wish to consider rotating the Service Manager position from time to time to keep new ideas flowing.

Fg. 9   **Key Roles in ITSM**

service sponsor   **service manager**   **service team**

- Sets budget for project
- Assesses risk
- Establishes service-level target

- Understands customer expectations
- Understands how service is supported and delivered
- Oversees critical processes such as Change Management and Incident Management

- Ensures ongoing service efficacy
- Recommends service improvements and identifies expansion opportunities
- Contributes to Service Catalog

| 9 |

IT Governance

In Chapter 3, we introduced a multitude of other ITSM systems that can be used in lieu of ITIL or as a supplement. Among these systems was COBIT 5, which places particular emphasis on distinguishing "IT Governance" from "IT Management." While both of these terms are used frequently outside of COBIT, COBIT provides a delineation scheme that serves to highlight core qualities of each pursuit (governance and management). The lines of separation are drawn along purpose, responsibilities, types of activities, and supporting organizational structures. COBIT introduces the following mnemonics:

Fg. 10

IT Governance	IT Management
Evaluate	**Plan**
Direct	**Build**
Monitor	**Run**
	Monitor

Overall, IT governance is more concerned with the setting of standards and objectives, whereas IT management is tasked with execution. COBIT further defines a multitude of processes that IT departments may choose to access (on a line-item basis) when undertaking their governance and management efforts.

IT governance has a strong influence in determining how the performance of your IT department will be measured. Good governance ensures that IT standards support business needs (as is germane to the running theme of ITSM). Governance should also dictate where measuring points should be located within the IT organization. For example, if the focus of the business is to be the best web-hosting service in the region or worldwide, then IT governance must establish evaluation points that speak to this goal. The percentage of server uptime might be a worthy metric to consider, as would be feedback from customers who use the service and are prepared to endorse it as reliable. Data security is another concern that often falls within the purview of IT governance. Is company data accessible to unauthorized parties? Have there been any leaks in private customer information? Is all sensitive data possessed by the company secured to the proper standard?

IT governance is also used to keep tabs on budgetary matters. There should be a system set up that governs (monitors) IT spending. IT governance ensures that IT spending is justified in proportion to the business needs it services. When new IT resources are purchased to fulfill an IT management objective, the dollar figures must pass the scrutiny of the IT department's governing apparatus.

IT governance standards can also be applied to disaster planning. In a worst-case scenario, where a security failure or service failure compromises the integrity of the operation and interrupts service to customers, how long will it take for the system to be recovered? What's the extent of the potential damage to the company's welfare? IT governance should establish clear damage-control bright lines. A good example of this use of IT governance is data security in the banking industry, where critical financial records are stored on servers. IT governance sets standards for backup redundancy, ensuring that a massive data calamity would never leave critical records completely unrecoverable.

Though we've discussed many of the urgent needs for IT governance, it's important to recognize that IT governance is also used to help a business define and position itself in the market. For example, if your company is dead set on building a reputation as having the most responsive service desk, then you should use IT governance to establish and monitor incident resolution times. If your company operates an internet-based stock trading platform and earns commissions on every trade, then you will use IT governance to set a particular threshold for the specific number of trades you need to process in a given day. This is where IT governance meets business service head-on. If you're looking for a way to get management to take the needs of IT more seriously, then align your IT governance standards directly with sales goals.

Note : *Commissioned stock trades are essentially sales for the broker.*

In *Service Management for Dummies*, authors Judith Hurwitz et al. argue that IT managers fare better when they proactively integrate IT with business interests, as opposed to waiting for an IT shortcoming to negatively affect business. "You certainly will hear [about it] loud and clear when a service failure leads to business disruptions."[18]

The combined utility of IT governance as a cost-monitoring and service-enhancing endeavor can have a tremendous impact on business vitality. When done correctly, IT governance will boost an organization's return on assets (net income divided by total assets).

It Gets Easier

When you first implement IT governance at your organization it may seem tedious to maintain: keeping track of all the regulations, recording all the metrics, etc. As time passes, however, and your IT governance systems mature, you will notice that things tend to

---

[18] Hurwitz et al, "Service Management For Dummies," 114.

streamline and get a lot easier. The trick is identifying those core measuring points that are the most useful and then developing a flexible and accurate way to keep track of them.

Governance & Compliance

Depending on the type of business and the applicable local, state, and federal laws, certain compliance practices may be required. These practices can involve record keeping, safety, security, or other aspects of your business that somehow have the potential to impact the greater world. IT governance is the natural ally of compliance. When you define IT governance, it's a lot like defining corporate policy, but limited to the realm of IT.

The good news is that technology, if properly configured, can't willfully behave in a way contrary to applicable compliance standards. The bad news is that you may often find yourself in the unenviable position of causing short-term pain for longer-term well-being. Compliance activities are often costly and don't directly benefit immediate business concerns. Other members of your organization may resent your efforts to assure compliance, but these are the same people who'd want your head on a platter if a bad audit led to their jobs (or even their freedom) being put at risk.

| 10 |

ITSM & Security

When attempting to integrate a good security protocol into your ITSM efforts, you have several resources available. ITIL has a defined subprocess called "security management" (part of Service Design) that's devoted to ensuring that company and customer information is properly protected.

If you're quite keen on enforcing ongoing security standards within your organization, then you can take advantage of the stringent checklists found in the ISO 20000 framework.

Note : ISO 27000 is the specific section dealing with security of information assets.

As hackers continue to become more sophisticated, more and more money continues to be invested in information security. This is in stark contrast to the minimal amount of security expenditure pre-internet. Security is another highly tricky facet of ITSM. It's difficult to prove that a security system is working. It may seem as if it's doing nothing when, in reality, it's blocking many dangerous attacks. When pursuing ITSM principles, we're engaging in a constant effort to show how IT is creating real business value. When it comes to security, IT professionals are again somewhat caught in the middle—they're not going to get much credit for preventing things that never happen, but should they fail to prevent a security breach and adverse consequences ensue, they will be quick to the chopping block.

But there's no reason to get too glum about the situation. In this day and age most everyone has some sympathy for the need for security when safeguarding vast and sensitive data. There are also a multitude of practices you can adopt that will help secure data while also supporting business service goals. One such fitting example was discussed in Chapter 5, where we reviewed a scenario in which service customers had acquired a problematic habit of continually losing their log-in passwords. The response was to require a manual password reset every month, which forced each customer to keep regular tabs on their own password. The end result was that both a service objective and a security objective were advanced.

There are other ways in which security enhancements can improve service, or at least not interfere with it. Some companies use **white lists** to dictate what software and apps may be run in various sectors of the IT setup. Anything that doesn't show up on the white list is not allowed to run; therefore, any attempt by an outside party to run an unauthorized program will be unsuccessful.

Most companies rely on one or more types of identity verification protocols to control which employees have access to various software components. The general preference is to give employees access to data on a need-to-have basis. This can be readily accomplished by creating separate log-in gateways for each branch of the IT apparatus. Though the numbers aren't absolute, it's widely thought that most security breaches in a business IT department involve an insider accomplice. Someone inside the company opens a back door to facilitate the intrusion. This could be as simple as giving someone their password. If the intrusion comes from a computer outside the company, then it's often quite difficult to prove that the insider accomplice had anything to do with the attack.

On other occasions, attackers may not need any support from an inside party. Hacking has developed and expanded into a profitable trade over the years. Hackers are often able to utilize the computing power of thousands and thousands of compromised computers to run sophisticated programs designed to break through firewalls and harvest valuable, sensitive data. And it's certainly not unheard of for one organization to hire a hacker to compromise the data security of a competitor. Trade secrets, financial information, customer data, marketing data—they can be quite valuable in the right hands, and there's no shortage of aspiring hackers willing to facilitate these illicit transfers.

The practice of encryption has been featured widely in the news in recent months. Companies like WhatsApp have allowed customers to encrypt data to protect their privacy. Meanwhile, the service has been exploited by terrorist and crime organizations. The reality of encryption is that it does make data intrusion a whole lot less profitable for intruders. They may be successful in obtaining sensitive data from you, but what good does it do them if they can't read it? Keep in mind, however, that encryption will drain your resources and slow down the processing and transfer of the data. For this reason, a lot of companies delineate various bodies of data for encryption while leaving other data unencrypted.

Government agencies and companies that suspect industrial espionage sometimes use countermeasures that detect and attempt to reveal the whereabouts of digital intruders. One such countermeasure is known as "spoofing" and involves baiting an attacker with a false website, email address, or IP address. Spoofing can also be used to ward off attacks that are attempting to identify systems that use specific versions of software, usually those with known vulnerabilities or those that are likely to contain valuable data. Spoofing can be used to provide the hacker with false information, making the business's servers appear to be of little interest.

Know the Enemy : Logging Is Power

One of the simplest ways to safeguard your IT department from intrusions is to maintain an activity log record for critical software components such as your firewall, operating system, and databases. You will find that these components have the ability to track attempted access and to issue red-flag alerts when out-of- the-ordinary activity is detected. The log information could shed some light on how and when your data is being targeted for attack. Unfortunately, most attackers are careful to safeguard their identities, so you're unlikely to discover the identity of the culprit. But if you can identify the type of attack being pursued, then you will be able to respond in kind.

Going Old School

Don't forget that the most obvious way to steal data from an IT department is to simply walk in the front door, pick up a couple of servers, and walk out. Make sure you have sufficient physical security resources in place, up to and including security alarms and guards.

ITIL's Security KPIs

The information security ITIL sub-task uses a system of six different key performance indicators (KPIs) to monitor effectiveness. You'll find a more extensive list of standards in the ISO 20000 framework, but the ITIL KPIs will get you off to the right start in maintaining secure data.

KPI 1 – Number of Implemented Preventative Measures

This KPI charts the number of security measures that have been implemented in response to a perceived vulnerability, a known intrusion attempt, or a successful intrusion. In order for this KPI to have any meaning it needs to be traced back to a need that's justifiably identified in your particular data system.

KPI 2 – Implementation Duration

This KPI tracks the time between the point at which a justified security concern is identified and the point in time when an appropriate resolution is put into place.

KPI 3 – Number of Major Security Incidents

This KPI tracks the number of security incidents and assigns each incident a specific severity level.

KPI 4 – Number of Security-Related Service Downtimes

This KPI tracks the number of times that a security concern prevented service from being available to customers.

KPI 5 – Number of Security Tests

This KPI tracks the number of proactive steps that the IT department has taken to measure existing data security, such as tests and trainings.

KPI 6 – Number of Identified Shortcomings during Security Tests

This KPI takes the measurements quantified in KPI 5 and plots them against the shortcomings that were identified during the tests.

By using these ITIL KPIs for the information security management subprocess, IT managers can not only better monitor their data security, but they can also introduce compelling data to business managers to justify investment in new and better security defenses and countermeasures.

conclusion

Some ITSM concepts can be taught, while a vast assortment of other things must be experienced and learned directly. When developing an ITSM strategy for your organization, keep in mind the famous principle: "Give a man a fish, feed him for a day. Teach a man to fish, feed him for a lifetime." In order to be successful with ITSM, you must bring your team members on board and get them contributing as soon as possible. It's better to have a team in which 90% of the membership has a rudimentary understanding of what ITSM means, as opposed to a team in which 10% of the membership has an excellent understanding of what it means. Once your team begins understanding, buying in, and applying their talents to making your IT department more service-oriented, the true potential of ITSM will be unleashed and you'll begin to see the changes and the benefits.

Finally, don't write off the potential for positive impact that could result from involving an outside party in your ITSM training. Bringing in experienced parties to coach and help you plan your transition can mean the difference between remaining stagnant and moving your organization forward.

glossary

Business Process Framework (eTOM) -
The standard digital enterprise IT framework utilized primarily by the telecommunication and entertainment industry. The eTOM standard optimizes communication between various parties within the industry and allows for productive and agile business cooperation.

Capability Maturity Model (CMM) -
Created in 1986 by the Software Engineering Institute at Carnegie Mellon, the CMM model was originally used as an assessment tool for process maturity in software development but was soon expanded to encompass a variety of IT processes (see Process Maturity).

COBIT (Control Objectives for Information & Related Technology) -
Developed and overseen by the nonprofit ISACA (Information Systems Audit and Control Association), this tool set utilizes highly defined inputs and outputs that allow multiple IT operations to interact with utmost efficiency. Next to ITIL, COBIT is commonly thought to be the most important modern IT framework.

Configuration Management Database (CMDB) -
A "data warehouse" that stores the assets of an IT organization and defines the various relationships and communication channels shared between them.

Events -
Commonly referred to as an "event record," this refers to a change in state in an IT system that influences the configuration of a system or impacts a service. Events are usually logged and reported and may turn into "incidents" if they result in a disruption of service.

Incident -
An incident is declared when a service is interrupted or its quality is severely impaired.

Integration Infrastructure -
Middleware that allows multiple applications to communicate with one another.

ISO/IEC 20000 -
A prescriptive, easily measurable framework for IT performance. Unlike ITIL, ISO/IEC 20000 is designed to be easily auditable and verifiable, and is a good standard to use when enforcing basic competency thresholds in an IT organization.

IT Governance (ITG) -
Refers to the efficient, effective, and cost-sensitive application of IT to attain the business goals. ITG is broken up into two sides. Supply side ITG is primarily undertaken by a company or organization's CIO, and its purpose is to ensure that IT resources are being used effectively. Demand side governance refers to how organizations evaluate, plan, prioritize, and fund business needs that can be met through the application of IT.

ITIL -
A broad multivolume advisory guide containing a system of best practices for IT. Thought by many to be the established norm for the practice of IT.

ITIL Life Cycle Stages -
The five core broad-topic areas covered by ITIL v3 (2011): service strategy, service design, service transition, service operation, and continual service improvement. Each ITIL Life Cycle Stage relies on multiple processes and subprocesses to support its objectives.

ITSM -
Information Technology Service Management refers to the continual effort toward incorporating IT into the service needs of business.

IT Systems Management -
A broad bucket term referring to how an organization manages its IT assets. It is separate from ITSM (IT Service Management), which seeks to incorporate IT Systems Management into the service needs of a business or organization.

KPIs (Key Performance Indicators) -
In ITIL, KPIs are used to evaluate the quality of performance achieved through the use of various ITIL processes (see Process).

Maturity Model -
A blueprint for scrutinizing a process to allow it to grow more effective with time. (See Capability Maturity Model).

Network Management -
A system of activities and tools used to support and optimize computer network systems. ITSM seeks to incorporate Network Management practices into an intelligible, business service-oriented framework.

Project Portfolio Management (PPM) -
PPM contains guidance on how to prioritize and execute projects in an efficient manner. PPM also includes an analytical evaluation framework by which the strength of ongoing projects may be assessed.

Process -
In ITIL, a process is one among a collection of IT practices listed under one of the five Life Cycle Stages. Each process contains methodologies to achieve objectives that support the Service Life Cycle stage. Most es use KPIs to evaluate progress made toward these objectives.

Process Maturity -
The extent to which a process has proven useful, has acquired documentation, is repeatable, and is being steadily improved upon. The more of these favorable attributes present in a process, the more "mature" it is said to be.

Note : The "process" being assessed and improved through Process Maturity need not necessarily be a strictly defined "ITIL" process.

Scrum -

A style of project management whereby a team works toward a goal in short, iterative bursts. Hierarchical roles among team members are often disregarded when working on a scrum team.

Service Catalog -
The organized assortment of all business and IT services offered by an organization.

Service Desk -
A service desk, in ITIL, is defined as a direct communication channel between the IT department and the users of a service.

Subprocess -
In ITIL, most processes include a collection of subprocesses used to support the main process's objectives.

White List -
A security protocol where only certain applications (those specifically designated on the "white list") are allowed to operate and access data on certain servers.

about clydebank

We are a multi-media publishing company that provides reliable, high-quality, and easily accessible information to a global customer base. Developed out of the need for beginner-friendly content that can be accessed across multiple platforms, we deliver unbiased, up-to-date, information through our multiple product offerings.

Through our strategic partnerships with some of the world's largest retailers, we are able to simplify the learning process for customers around the world, providing our readers with an authoritative source of information for the subjects that matter to them. Our end-user focused philosophy puts the satisfaction of our customers at the forefront of our mission. We are committed to creating multi-media products that allow our customers to learn what they want, when they want, and how they want.

ClydeBank Technology is a division of the multimedia-publishing firm ClydeBank Media. ClydeBank Media's goal is to provide affordable, accessible information to a global market through different forms of media such as eBooks, paperback books and audio books. Company divisions are based on subject matter, each consisting of a dedicated team of researchers, writers, editors and designers.

For more information, please visit us at :
www.clydebankmedia.com
or contact *info@clydebankmedia.com*

Your world, simplified.

notes

STAY INFORMED

ClydeBank TECHNOLOGY | BLOG

Your Source for All Things Technology

Why Should I Sign Up for the Mailing List?

- Be the first to know about new products
- Receive exclusive promotions & discounts
- Get a $10 ClydeBank Media gift card!

Stay on top of the latest business trends by joining our free mailing list today at:

www.clydebankmedia.com/technology-blog

Made in the USA
Lexington, KY
21 April 2017